Knock-knock Jokes

by Judy Winter

www.raintreepublishers.co.uk
Visit our website to find out
more information about
Raintree books.

To order:
☎ Phone 0845 6044371
▤ Fax +44 (0) 1865 312263
✉ Email myorders@raintreepublishers.co.uk

Customers from outside the UK please telephone +44 1865 312262

Raintree is an imprint of Capstone Global
Library Limited, a company incorporated
in England and Wales having its registered
office at 7 Pilgrim Street, London, EC4V 6LB –
Registered company number: 6695582

Editor: Catherine Veitch
Designer: Ted Williams
Studio specialist: Sarah Schuette
Studio scheduler: Marcy Morin
Production Specialist: Eric Manske
Originated by Capstone Global Library Ltd
Printed and bound in China by Leo Paper
Products Ltd

ISBN 978 1 406 24262 1 (paperback)
16 15 14 13 12
10 9 8 7 6 5 4 3 2 1

British Library Cataloguing in Publication Data
A full catalogue record for this book is available
from the British Library.

Acknowledgements
The author and the publishers are grateful
to the following for permission to reproduce
copyright material: all photos by Heinemann
Raintree (Karon Dubke), except: Capstone Press:
p. 14 (Gary Sundermeyer); iStockphoto: p.
6 - elephant (Johan Swanepoel); Shutterstock:
pp. 22, cover - tank (Gary Blakeley), flag (Milos
Luzanin); background design (throughout).

Every effort has been made to contact copyright
holders of material reproduced in this book.
Any omissions will be rectified in subsequent
printings if notice is given to the publisher.

Disclaimer
All the internet addresses (URLs) given in this
book were valid at the time of going to press.
However, due to the dynamic nature of the
internet, some addresses may have changed,
or sites may have changed or ceased to
exist since publication. While the author and
publisher regret any inconvenience this may
cause readers, no responsibility for any such
changes can be accepted by either the author
or the publisher.

Contents

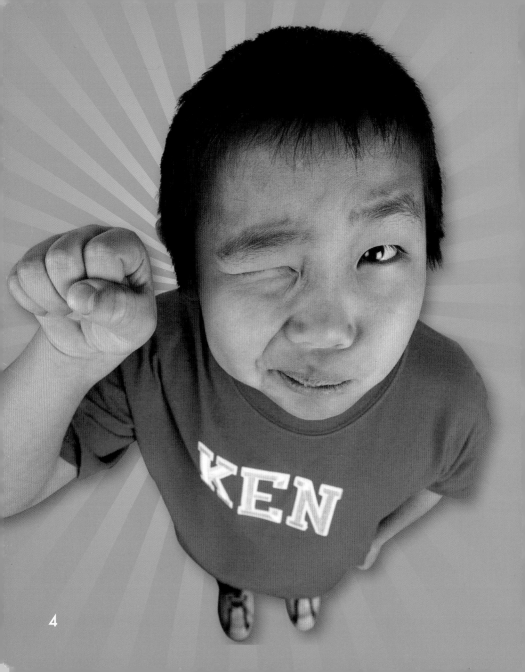

Knock, knock.

Who's there?

Ken.

Ken who?

Ken you let me in?

Knock, knock.

Who's there?

Les.

Les who?

Les go to the zoo!

Knock, knock.

Who's there?
Alma.

Alma who?
Alma sweets are gone!

Knock, knock.

Who's there?
Sarah.

Sarah who?
Sarah mouse in
your house?

Knock, knock.

Who's there?
Aardvark.

Aardvark who?
Aardvark a million
miles to see you.

14

Knock, knock.

Who's there?

Pig.

Pig who?

Pig up your feet
or you might trip.

Knock, knock.

Who's there?
Butter.

Butter who?
Butter watch your dog!

Knock, knock.

Who's there?
Ears.

Ears who?
Ears some more knock-knock jokes for you.

Knock, knock.

Who's there?
Woo.

Woo who?
You don't need to cheer. It's just a joke.

Knock, knock.

Who's there?
Tank.

Tank who?
You are welcome.

Further reading

Lettuce In! And other Knock-Knock Jokes (Little Simon Sillies), Tina Gallo (Simon and Schuster, 2011)

The Giggle-a-Day Joke Book, (Child of Achievement Awards) (HarperCollins, 2011)

Create your own joke

Follow these steps to write your own knock-knock joke:

1. Pick a name of, for example, a country or a person. Such as "Alaska".

2. Make a list of words or phrases that sound like or rhyme with the name. For example, "All ask her", "I'll ask her".

3. Try out different jokes, fitting your words from steps 1 and 2 into the knock-knock joke. For example,
"Knock, knock.
Who's there?
Alaska.
Alaska who?
Alaska my dad."